A Wee Worship Book

G-4425
$11.50

A Wee Worship Book

Fourth incarnation

WILD GOOSE WORSHIP GROUP

GIA Publications, Inc.
Chicago

First published 1999

ISBN 1 57999 061 4

Copyright © 1999 Wild Goose Resource Group

Front cover: Graham Maule © 1999 Wild Goose Resource Group

**Published and distributed in North America by GIA
Publications, Inc., 7404 S. Mason Ave., Chicago, IL 60638.
http://www.giamusic.com**

Printed by Bell & Bain, Thornliebank, Glasgow, Scotland

Contents

Introduction

Because the word *liturgy* originally meant 'the work of the people', this is a people's rather than a priest's or minister's book. It is not intended to replace denominational service books, but to enable people from a diversity of backgrounds to share forms of prayer which are not bound to the canons or sensitivities of one Christian tradition.

This is, in fact, the fourth incarnation of *A Wee Worship Book*. Its origins go back to a missionary conference in the mid-1980s, where a well-meaning cleric solemnly advised us that the title was inappropriate. We disregarded his comments after the first edition and, ever since, the book has been widely used throughout Great Britain and abroad.

Some of the liturgies have been published before but most of them have been produced in the past five years. And all have been amended in the light of comment and experience. We offer them to Christians in and on the fringe of the Church with gratitude for the insights, advice and encouragement given to us since the book first appeared without its diminutive title.

John L. Bell
Mairi Munro

for the Wild Goose Worship Group

Using the liturgies

Even if you never read forewords, please read this.

It would be impossible to list here everything that enables a fulfilling worship experience, but the following might be helpful, especially to those who are used to 'leading from the front'.

1. Planning

God honours our preparation, and our preparation honours God. Looking up a liturgy five minutes before the time for evening prayer, and asking the gathering people what their favourite hymns are shows both a low opinion of corporate worship and, worse, a low opinion of God to whom worship is offered.

So, take time with other people, to think through what will be used, who will lead, where the worship will happen and how it will be introduced.

If announcements have to be made, or instructions given regarding conversations in worship or engaging in symbolic action, rehearse the announcements, ensuring they are concise and clear rather than off-the-cuff and rambling.

2. Leadership

With the exception of the orders for Holy Communion, it is presumed that anyone who wishes should be able to lead these liturgies. At the same time, it is also envisaged that no one voice should predominate. So while one person may be the anchor who introduces the liturgy and perhaps leads the opening and closing responses, others may lead the prayers, read scripture, etc.

Particularly in the matter of leading prayer, if the space has a good acoustic, or if all worshippers have copies of the book, there is no need for the prayers to be led from a lectern. Some people who have an understandable reticence about standing up in front will happily read from among or behind the congregation. However, as a rule of thumb, it is best to ask such leaders, who read from the periphery of the group, to stand, and to speak into the middle of the assembly.

3. Environment

Where we worship can often dictate or influence *how* we worship.

If people are scattered throughout a large church with yards of empty pews between them, we are not the Body of Christ. We are a gathering of strangers who give the impression to the outsider that we do not belong to each other.

So, for these liturgies we may want to consider how and where we sit, remembering that a circular or semi-circular formation round a table is more symbolic of Christian fellowship than straight lines facing a lectern.

Lighting is also important. There is no need to burn every lamp if only a section of the space is being used. Candles and darkness help to create intimacy. It is also helpful to have a focal point – such as a cross or large candle on which people may rest their eyes.

If people are expected to move during worship, thought should be given to what enables that. Plenty of corridor space, small groups of chairs and music being sung or played all help; long rows, narrow pews and silence can intimidate.

4. Music

Nearly all the singing of the Wild Goose Worship Group is unaccompanied. This is neither because we disparage instruments nor because we are skilled vocalists – far from it. It is simply because we believe in the value of the human voice and that the Church's worship is the place in which it should be liberated and not constrained. All our experience in Britain, Europe, North America, and in the Southern Hemisphere confirms that when people are expected to sing, they will; where it is inferred that they 'might not manage it', they don't.

So be prepared, in charity, to encourage musicians sometimes to leave the keyboard or the fretboard, pitch the first note and let the people sing. And because it is not envisaged that this book will be used primarily in regular Sunday worship, do not feel compelled to have music played before or after. Let the worshippers set the tone, not the organ or the praise band.

We have not included a selection of the songs we use, although they are mentioned in an index. But we have included some of the simplest chants which we teach congregations to sing in parts and without music. Those who find this most difficult are those who usually read music.

5. The Bible

If you are going to read the Bible, practise reading aloud in your bedroom before you ever do it in worship. People can only hear God's word if it is read well. This does not mean that reading is only for those who have gone to elocution or are amateur dramatics enthusiasts. It does mean that whatever is meant to be heard by others has to be read intelligibly.

The interpretation of scripture does not begin with the homily or sermon; it begins when the reader convincingly communicates the vitality of God's word.

6. Conversations

Several of the liturgies suggest optional conversation on the passages of scripture which have been read. Just as some musicians disbelieve that those who don't read music can ever sing on their own or sing in harmony, so some ministers and priests suspect the ability of untrained lay people to discuss the Bible intelligently.

As long as leaders have a 'right answers' mentality, or want to be the arbiters of proper biblical interpretation, their apprehensions will be fulfilled. But if people are invited to discuss their reactions, their insights, their vague ideas, rather than state definitive opinions, discussion of scripture can be very illuminating.

The doubters should look at a volume of the *Solentiname Gospels*, reflections of peasants in Nicaragua on the Gospel stories as enabled by a priest. These contain more insights into the relevance of the Bible to daily living than any number of academic commentaries.

7. Symbolic action

We encourage the occasional use of symbolic action both because God engages in symbolic action to communicate with humanity, and because not everyone is fulfilled by words alone.

At the same time, we appreciate that for some people – and for reasons that cannot always be articulated – symbolic action, whether lighting a candle or planting a seed, is difficult. Our experience is that where such activity is always clearly stated as *optional*, and people are not coerced into doing that which is against their instincts, there is little dissension. Rather – as with raising hands in worship or dancing – those who refrain can be appreciative of those who participate.

In this book the activities suggested are fairly straightforward in comparison to what we might suggest in services of worship focusing on one particular theme, and all should be manageable in most situations.

8. Holy Communion

There are two orders provided. The first is the longer of the two and has in mind a large assembly. The shorter order is also usable in large gatherings, but was originally intended for a more domestic setting.

Different Christian traditions have their own special emphases regarding the celebration of the Eucharist. The location of the Peace in the liturgy, the inclusion of eucharistic acclamations, the way in which the people receive and the way in which the bread and wine are presented – all such issues find a variety of expression throughout Christendom.

It is therefore up to the local community to adopt and adapt as suits their purpose, all the time recognising that Communion is not the property of the Church, but the gift of God. And that no celebration of Catholic Mass, Holy Communion or Lord's Supper perfectly replicates what Jesus did in an upstairs room.

Morning liturgy A

This liturgy, like others in this collection, offers an OPTIONAL CONVERSATION after the reading of the WORD OF GOD. In some situations this may be more manageable and appropriate than in others. If the conversation is to be used, it is helpful to tell people in advance, and reassure them that this is a free-ranging and open conversation, not an academic exercise.

Where the morning liturgies are used to start a day's work, people may move, where appropriate, immediately from the CLOSING RESPONSES to the next activity, thus indicating that God is with us as much in our daily work as in the worship space.

Silence or gathering song

Call to worship   *(ALL standing)*

Leader:	In the beginning before time, before people, before the world began,
ALL:	GOD WAS.

Leader:	Here and now among us, beside us, enlisting the people of earth for the purposes of heaven,
ALL:	GOD IS.

Leader:	In the future, when we have turned to dust and all we know has found its fulfilment,
ALL:	GOD WILL BE.

Leader:	Not denying the world, but delighting in it, not condemning the world, but redeeming it, through Jesus Christ, by the power of the Holy Spirit,

ALL: GOD WAS,
          GOD IS,
          GOD WILL BE.

A song of praise

Prayer   *(ALL seated)*

Leader: Let us pray.

          In you, gracious God,
          the widowed find a carer,
          the orphaned find a parent,
          the fearful find a friend.

          In you,
          the wounded find a healer,
          the penitent find a pardoner,
          the burdened find a counsellor.

          In you,
          the miserly find a beggar,
          the despondent find a laughter-maker,
          the legalists find a rule-beaker.

          In you, Jesus Christ,
          we meet our Maker,
          and our match.

          And if some need to say, 'Help me'
          and if some need to say, 'Save me'
          and if some need to say, 'Hold me'
          and if some need to say, 'Forgive me'
          then let these be said now
          in confidence
          by us.

          (Silence)

O Christ,
in whose heart is both welcome and warning,
say to us,
do to us,
reveal within us
the things that will make us whole.

And we will wait;
and we will praise you.
Amen.

Word of God

*(This may be prefaced by a sung acclamation such as
the DUNCAN ALLELUIA or the Caribbean HALLE,
HALLE, HALLE – see Appendix, pages 112 & 120.
People should stand or sit according to local custom)*

Reader: Hear the word of God.
ALL: OUR EARS ARE OPEN.
Reader: A reading from ...

(A portion of the scripture is read)

Reader: This is the Word of the Lord/Gospel of our Lord.
ALL: THANKS BE TO GOD.

(The acclamation may be repeated)

Optional conversation

*(This conversation should be open-ended. People may be
invited to turn to each other in small groups and share
their response to the questions below. No feedback is
necessary. The conversations may be concluded by the
singing of the acclamation, which is now familiar)*

Leader: Let us reflect together on what we have heard, by
responding to these two questions:

1. What words in that reading do I particularly remember and why?

2. Was the reading intended to have an effect on what I think, what I do or what I believe?

Prayers of the people

Leader: Let us pray for the breaking in of God's kingdom in our world today.

Lord God,
because Jesus has taught us to trust you in all things,
we hold to his word and share his plea:
ALL: YOUR KINGDOM COME, YOUR WILL BE DONE.

Leader: Where nations budget for war,
while Christ says, 'Put up your sword':
ALL: YOUR KINGDOM COME, YOUR WILL BE DONE.

Leader: Where countries waste food and covet fashion,
while Christ says, 'I was hungry ... I was thirsty ... ':
ALL: YOUR KINGDOM COME, YOUR WILL BE DONE.

Leader: Where powerful governments
claim their policies are heaven blessed,
while scripture states
that God helps the powerless:
ALL: YOUR KINGDOM COME, YOUR WILL BE DONE.

Leader: Where Christians seek the kingdom
in the shape of their own church,
as if Christ had come to build
and not to break barriers:
ALL: YOUR KINGDOM COME, YOUR WILL BE DONE.

Leader: Where women who speak up for their dignity
are treated with scorn or contempt:
ALL: YOUR KINGDOM COME, YOUR WILL BE DONE.

Leader:	Where men try hard to be tough,
	because they're afraid to be tender:
ALL:	YOUR KINGDOM COME, YOUR WILL BE DONE.

Leader:	Where we, obsessed with being adult,
	forget to become like children:
ALL:	YOUR KINGDOM COME, YOUR WILL BE DONE.

Leader:	Where our prayers falter,
	our faith weakens,
	our light grows dim:
ALL:	YOUR KINGDOM COME, YOUR WILL BE DONE.

Leader:	Where Jesus Christ calls us:
ALL:	YOUR KINGDOM COME, YOUR WILL BE DONE.

Leader:	Lord God,
	you have declared that your kingdom is among us.
	Open our ears to hear it,
	our hands to serve it,
	our hearts to hold it.
	This we pray in Jesus' name.
ALL:	AMEN.

Song or hymn

Closing responses   *(ALL standing)*

Leader:	For all that God can do within us,
	for all that God can do without us,
ALL:	THANKS BE TO GOD.

Leader:	For all in whom Christ lived before us,
	for all in whom Christ lives beside us,
ALL:	THANKS BE TO GOD.

Leader:	For all the Spirit wants to bring us,
	for where the Spirit wants to send us,
ALL:	THANKS BE TO GOD.
Leader:	Listen,
	Christ has promised to be with us
	in the world as in our worship.
ALL:	AMEN.
	WE GO TO SERVE HIM.

Morning liturgy B

In the OPENING AFFIRMATION, it is suggested that men and women alternate. Where the company is predominantly one gender, it may be more sensitive to divide people into two groups, according to seating, thus still enabling the responses to be said antiphonally.

In the intercessory PRAYERS, anyone may say a name aloud at the appropriate time. If this has never been done before, people should be aware of this possibility before the liturgy begins.

Opening affirmation   *(ALL standing)*

Leader:	Among the poor,
	among the proud,
Men:	among the persecuted
Women:	among the privileged,
ALL:	CHRIST IS COMING TO MAKE ALL THINGS NEW.

Leader:	In the private house,
	in the public place,
Men:	in the wedding feast
Women:	in the judgement hall,
ALL:	CHRIST IS COMING TO MAKE ALL THINGS NEW.

Leader:	With a gentle touch,
	with an angry word,
Men:	with a clear conscience,
Women:	with burning love,
ALL:	CHRIST IS COMING TO MAKE ALL THINGS NEW.

Leader:	That the kingdom might come,
	that the world might believe,
Men:	that the powerful might stumble,
Women:	that the hidden might be seen,
ALL:	CHRIST IS COMING TO MAKE ALL THINGS NEW.

Leader:	Within us, without us,
	behind us, before us,
Men:	in this place, in every place,
Women:	for this time, for all time,
ALL:	CHRIST IS COMING TO MAKE ALL THINGS NEW.

Song or hymn

Prayer   *(ALL seated)*

Leader: Let us pray.

Because you made the world,
and intended it to be a good place,
and called its people your children;
because, when things seemed at their worst,
you came in Christ to bring out the best in us;
so, gracious God, we gladly say:

ALL: GOODNESS IS STRONGER THAN EVIL,
LOVE IS STRONGER THAN HATE,
LIGHT IS STRONGER THAN DARKNESS.
TRUTH IS STRONGER THAN LIES.

Leader: Because confusion can reign inside us,
despite our faith;
because anger, tension, bitterness and envy
distort our vision;
because our minds sometimes worry small things
out of all proportion;
because we do not always get it right,
we want to believe:

ALL: GOODNESS IS STRONGER THAN EVIL,
LOVE IS STRONGER THAN HATE,
LIGHT IS STRONGER THAN DARKNESS.
TRUTH IS STRONGER THAN LIES.

Leader: Because you have promised to hear us,
and are able to change us,
and are willing to make our hearts your home,
we ask you to confront,
control, forgive and encourage us,
as you know best.

(Pause)

Then let us cherish in our hearts
that which we proclaim with our lips:
ALL: GOODNESS IS STRONGER THAN EVIL,
LOVE IS STRONGER THAN HATE,
LIGHT IS STRONGER THAN DARKNESS.
TRUTH IS STRONGER THAN LIES.

Leader: Lord, hear our prayer,
and change our lives
until we illustrate the grace
of the God who makes all things new.
ALL: AMEN.

Word of God

Reader: In the beginning was the Word
ALL: AND THE WORD WAS WITH GOD,
AND THE WORD WAS GOD.

Reader: A reading from ... chapter ... verse ...

(The scripture is read)

Reader: For the Word of God is scripture,
for the Word of God is among us,
for the Word of God is within us;
ALL: THANKS BE TO GOD.

Optional conversation

(The form of conversation used in MORNING LITURGY
A on page 13–14 may also be used here)

Prayers

Leader: Let us pray.

Holy God,
though this world depends on your grace,
it is governed and tended by mortals.

So we pray for those
who walk the corridors of power
in the parliaments of this and other lands,
whose judgements we value or fear.

(Names may be said aloud)

May they always consider those they represent,
make decisions with courage and integrity,
and resist any temptation
to abuse the trust placed in them.

Lord hear us.
ALL: LORD GRACIOUSLY HEAR US.

Leader: We pray for those who hold key positions
in the worlds of finance, business and industry,
whose decisions may profit some
or impoverish many.

(Names may be said aloud)

May they always value people higher than profit;
may they never impose burdens on the poor
which they would not carry themselves;
and may they never divorce money from morality
or ownership from stewardship.

Lord hear us,
ALL: LORD GRACIOUSLY HEAR US.

Leader: We pray for those in the caring professions,
who look after and listen to
kind, cruel and cantankerous folk,
and for those who make decisions
regarding the nation's health and welfare.

(Names may be said aloud)

May they always sense the sanctity of life
and every person's uniqueness;
may they help and heal
by their interest as well as their skill;
and may they be saved from tiredness
and an excess of demands.

Lord hear us.

ALL: LORD GRACIOUSLY HEAR US.

Leader: And let us remember
those for whom we are responsible
and to whom we are accountable
in what we do today.

(Names may be said aloud)

May we show to them
the thoughtfulness, tolerance
and kindness of Jesus.

Lord hear us

ALL: LORD GRACIOUSLY HEAR US.

Leader: Lord, hear our prayers,
and if today we might be the means
by which you answer the prayers of others,
then may you find us
neither deaf nor defiant,
but keen to fulfil your purpose,
for Jesus' sake.

ALL: AMEN.

A song or hymn *(ALL standing)*

Closing responses

Leader: From where we are
to where you need us,
ALL: JESUS, NOW LEAD ON.

Leader: From the security of what we know
to the adventure of what you will reveal,
ALL: JESUS, NOW LEAD ON.

Leader: To refashion the fabric of this world
until it resembles the shape of your kingdom,
ALL: JESUS NOW LEAD ON.

Leader: Because good things have been prepared
for those who love God,
ALL: JESUS NOW LEAD ON.

Morning liturgy C

In this liturgy, more flexibility is offered regarding the intercessory PRAYERS FOR THE DAY. A very basic pattern is outlined which may be amended or omitted ad lib. Where people have a reluctance to pray aloud in worship, silent prayer should be encouraged, and – at least in this case – the silences should be more than the cursory five seconds.

Opening responses *(ALL standing)*

Leader: O God, you summon the day to dawn,
           you teach the morning to waken the earth.
ALL: GREAT IS YOUR NAME.
           GREAT IS YOUR LOVE.

Leader: For you the valleys shall sing for joy,
           the trees of the field shall clap their hands.
ALL: GREAT IS YOUR NAME.
           GREAT IS YOUR LOVE.

Leader: For you the monarchs of the earth shall bow,
           the poor and persecuted shall shout for joy.
ALL: GREAT IS YOUR NAME.
           GREAT IS YOUR LOVE.

Leader: Your love and mercy shall last for ever,
           fresh as the morning, sure as the sunrise.
ALL: GREAT IS YOUR NAME.
           GREAT IS YOUR LOVE.

A song or hymn

Prayer   *(ALL sit)*

Leader: Let us pray.

Lord God,
early in the morning,
when the world was young,
you made life in all its beauty and terror,
you gave birth to all that we know.

Hallowed be your name.

ALL: HALLOWED BE YOUR NAME.

Leader: Early in the morning,
when the world least expected it,
a newborn child crying in a cradle
announced that you had come among us,
that you were one of us.

Hallowed be your name.

ALL: HALLOWED BE YOUR NAME.

Leader: Early in the morning,
surrounded by respectable liars,
religious leaders, anxious statesmen
and silent friends,
you accepted the penalty for doing good,
for being God:
you shouldered and suffered the cross.

Hallowed be your name

ALL: HALLOWED BE YOUR NAME.

Leader: Early in the morning
a voice in a guarded graveyard
and footsteps in the dew
proved that you had risen,
that you came back
to those and for those
who had forgotten, denied and destroyed you.

Hallowed be your name.

ALL: HALLOWED BE YOUR NAME.

Leader: Early in the morning
in the multicoloured company
of your Church on earth and in heaven
we celebrate your creation,
your life,
your death and resurrection,
your interest in us:
so to you we pray,

ALL: LORD, BRING NEW LIFE
WHERE WE ARE WORN AND TIRED,
NEW LOVE
WHERE WE HAVE TURNED HARD-HEARTED,
FORGIVENESS
WHERE WE FEEL HURT
AND WHERE WE HAVE WOUNDED,
AND THE JOY AND FREEDOM
OF YOUR HOLY SPIRIT
WHERE WE ARE THE PRISONERS OF OURSELVES.

(Silence)

Leader: To all and to each
where regret is real,
God pronounces pardon
and grants us the right to begin again.

Thanks be to God!

ALL: AMEN.

Word of God

*(This may be preceded and/or followed by a song,
chorus or chant)*

Leader: The scripture reading is found in ... chapter ... verse ...

Let us listen for the Word of the Lord.

(Scripture is read)

	This is the Word/Gospel of the/our Lord.
ALL:	THANKS BE TO GOD.

Prayers for the day

Leader: Let us prepare ourselves for the day before us,
and claim its potential sent by God.

Let us pray.

We bring to God our concerns for today ...

*(These may be expressed ad lib. by anyone, ending with
an agreed phrase, e.g. Lord, in your mercy, hear our
prayer. If using this phrase, it could alternatively be sung
– see Appendix, page 125)*

Leader: We bring to God the people of today ...

(Free prayer as before)

Leader: And let us pray for ourselves ...

(Free prayer as before)

Leader: Lord, give us wisdom before we speak,
understanding while we listen,
sensitivity towards those we meet,
and the perspective of your kingdom
in which to see the things of the earth.

Bring us to the day's ending
blessed through having shared the day's beginning.
In Christ's name we ask this.
Amen.

Song   *(ALL standing)*

Blessing

Leader: May God bless us;
               may God keep us in the Spirit's care
               and lead our lives with love.

ALL: MAY CHRIST'S WARM WELCOME
               SHINE FROM OUR HEARTS
               AND CHRIST'S OWN PEACE PREVAIL
               THROUGH THIS AND EVERY DAY,
               TILL GREATER LIFE SHALL CALL.
               AMEN.

Morning liturgy D

In the Western Highlands and Islands of Scotland, prayer in the ancient Celtic tradition was on the verge of disappearing when Alexander Carmichael gathered prayers, songs and sayings from country folk and published them in CARMINA GADELICA (SONGS OF THE GAELS) at the end of the 19th century.

This liturgy uses material from that collection of fragments. What is of special interest is that few, if any, of these prayers came from ministers or priests. They were shared in families through the centuries by people who lived often without the benefit of clergy, yet believed deeply and prayed reverently.

Opening responses   *(ALL standing)*

Leader: Thanks be to you, O God,
                  that we have risen this day
ALL: TO THE RISING OF THIS LIFE ITSELF.

Leader: Be the purpose of God
                  between us and each purpose,
ALL: THE HAND OF GOD
                  BETWEEN US AND EACH HAND.

Leader: The pain of Christ
                  between us and each pain,
ALL: THE LOVE OF CHRIST
                  BETWEEN US AND EACH LOVE.

Leader: O God, who brought us
                  to the bright light of this new day
ALL: BRING US TO THE GUIDING LIGHT
                  OF ETERNITY.

Hymn

Prayer   *(ALL remain standing)*

Leader: God of life, do not darken your light to us,
Men: God of life do not limit your joy in us,
Women: God of life, do not shut your door to us,
Leader: God of life, do not refuse us your mercy,
ALL: LORD, DO NOT REFUSE US YOUR MERCY.

Leader: Let us pray. *(ALL sit or kneel)*

                   O God of life,
                   eternity cannot hold you,
                   nor can our little words catch
                   the magnificence of your kindness.
                   Yet in the space of our small hearts
                   and in silence
                   you can come close and repair us.

                   (Silence)

Leader: O God of life,
                   grant us your forgiveness
ALL: FOR OUR CARELESS THOUGHTS,
                   FOR OUR THOUGHTLESS DEEDS,
                   FOR OUR EMPTY SPEECH
                   AND THE WORDS WITH WHICH
                   WE WOUNDED.

                   (Silence)

Leader: O God of life,
                   grant us your forgiveness,
ALL: FOR OUR FALSE DESIRES,
                   FOR OUR HATEFUL ACTIONS,
                   FOR OUR WASTEFULNESS
                   AND FOR ALL WE LEFT UNTENDED.

                   (Silence)

Leader: O loving Christ,
hanged on a tree
yet risen in the morning,
scatter the sin from our souls
as the mist from the hills;
begin what we do,
inform what we say,
redeem who we are.

ALL: IN YOU WE PLACE OUR HOPE,
OUR GREAT HOPE, OUR LIVING HOPE,
THIS DAY AND EVERMORE
AMEN.

Word of God

Leader: Listen for the Word which God has spoken;
ALL: SPEAK, LORD, TO OUR SPEAKING,
SPEAK, LORD, TO OUR LISTENING,
SPEAK, LORD, TO OUR SOULS'
DEEP UNDERSTANDING.

(After a pause, the portion of scripture is read slowly)

Affirmation *(ALL standing)*

Leader: We believe, O God of all gods,
that you are the eternal maker of life:
we believe, O God of all gods,
that you are the eternal maker of love.

ALL: WE BELIEVE,
O LORD AND GOD OF ALL PEOPLE,
THAT YOU ARE THE CREATOR
OF THE HIGH HEAVENS,
THAT YOU ARE THE CREATOR
OF THE SKIES ABOVE,
THAT YOU ARE THE CREATOR
OF THE OCEANS BELOW.

Leader: We believe, O Lord and God of all people,
that you are the one who created our souls
and set their course,
that you are the one who created our bodies
from dust and from ashes,
that you gave to our bodies their breath
and to our souls their possession.

ALL: GOD, BLESS TO US OUR BODIES,
GOD, BLESS TO US OUR SOULS,
GOD, BLESS TO US OUR LIVES,
GOD, BLESS TO US OUR BELIEF.

(ALL sit or kneel)

Prayer for the day

Leader: Let us pray.

Let us pray for those who may be born today
and bless them in Jesus' name.

(Pause)

The joy of God shine from your face
and joy to all who see you;
the shield of God surround your head,
and angels ever guard you.

ALL: MAY EVERY SEASON BE GOOD FOR YOU
AND THE SON OF MARY GIVE PEACE TO YOU.

Leader: Let us pray for those who must work today
and bless them in Jesus' name.

(Pause)

God bless to you today
the earth beneath your feet,
the path on which you tread,
the work of hand and mind,
the things which you desire.

ALL:
> AND WHEN THE DAY IS OVER,
> GOD BLESS TO YOU YOUR REST.

Leader:
> Let us pray for those who must travel today
> and bless them in Jesus' name.

> *(Pause)*

> May the keeping of Christ be round you,
> may the guarding of God be with you,
> to possess you, to protect you
> from danger and from loss.

ALL:
> MAY THE GOSPEL OF THE GOD OF GRACE
> BLESS YOU FROM HEAD TO SOLE.
> MAY THE GOSPEL OF THE KING OF HEAVEN
> BE WRAPPED AROUND YOUR BODY.

Leader:
> Let us pray for those who may face death today,
> and bless them in Jesus' name.

> *(Pause)*

> May God provide for you
> all that is needed
> for body, mind and soul
> as you face the final journey.

ALL:
> MAY CHRIST TAKE YOUR SOUL IN HIS ARMS,
> AND BRING YOU
> THROUGH THE BALANCING TIME
> TO THE DWELLING PLACE OF PEACE
> AND MAKE IT YOUR HOME FOR EVER.

Leader:
> And let us pray for ourselves.

ALL:
> ENABLE US, GREAT GOD,
> TO PASS THIS DAY
> AS PASS THE SAINTS IN HEAVEN,
> TO KEEP THIS DAY
> AS KEEP THE PEOPLE OF HEAVEN,
> TO SPEND THIS DAY
> AS SPEND THE HOUSEHOLD OF HEAVEN,

AND LOVE THIS DAY,
WHICH YOU HAVE PERFECTED.
AMEN.

A song or hymn *(Standing)*

The Peace

Leader: The peace of God,
the peace of God's people,
the peace of Mary mild, the loving one,
and of Christ, King of human hearts,
God's own peace ...

ALL: BE UPON EACH THING
OUR EYES TAKE IN,
BE UPON EACH THING
OUR EARS TAKE IN,
BE UPON OUR BODIES
WHICH COME FROM EARTH,
BE UPON OUR SOULS
WHICH COME FROM HEAVEN,
EVERMORE AND EVERMORE,
AMEN.

Morning liturgy E (Shorter order)

Although this is called a 'Shorter order', the length may seem at odds with the title. However, it should be noted that all the COLLECTS listed are not meant to be said one after the other; rather, a few can be chosen on any one occasion and read by different voices.

Opening responses   *(ALL standing)*

Leader: From the rising of the sun
              till its setting in the west,
ALL: GOD'S HOLY NAME BE PRAISED.

Leader: On the lips of children,
              by babies at the breast,
ALL: GOD'S HOLY NAME BE PRAISED.

Leader: In the visions of the old
              and the dreaming of the young,
ALL: GOD'S HOLY NAME BE PRAISED.

Leader: In the banquet hall of heaven
              and the forgotten corners of our hearts,
ALL: GOD'S HOLY NAME BE PRAISED.

Leader: Let all that has life and breath
              praise the Lord.
ALL: AMEN.
              WE PRAISE THE LORD!

Song of praise

Word of God

(ALL sit. A portion of scripture is read.)

Prayer

Leader: O God our Creator,
your kindness has brought us
the gift of a new morning.
Help us to leave yesterday,
and not to covet tomorrow
but to accept the uniqueness of today.

(Silence)

By your love
celebrated in your Word,
seen in your Son,
brought near by your Spirit,
take from us what we need to carry no longer,
so that we may be free again
to choose to serve you
and to be served by each other.

(Silence)

Cantor: Jesus Christ, Son of God, have mercy upon us
ALL: JESUS CHRIST, SON OF GOD,
HAVE MERCY UPON US

*(This response is sung repeatedly – for music see
Appendix, page 123. Alternatively, the Leader may read
the Cantor's line and the others say the response once
only. It is followed by a silence.)*

Leader: I believe that God forgives and sets us free
ALL: WE BELIEVE THAT GOD FORGIVES
AND SETS US FREE;
AND AT THE DAY'S BEGINNING,
WE COMMIT OURSELVES
TO FOLLOWING WHERE CHRIST CALLS
AND TO LOVING ONE ANOTHER.

Optional collects

(One or more of these collects from the world Church may be read, concluding with the BLESSING.)

A.   *(From the American Indian tradition)*

Lord, make our hearts places of peace
and our minds harbours of tranquillity.
Sow in our souls true love for you
and for one another;
and root deeply within us
friendship and unity,
and concord with reverence.
So may we give peace to each other sincerely
and receive it beautifully.

B.   *(From the Irish Celtic tradition)*

May the blessing of light be on us,
light without and light within.
May the blessed sun shine on us
and warm each heart
till it glows like a great fire,
so that strangers and friends
may come in and warm themselves.
And may the light shine out
from our eyes,
like a candle set in the windows of a house,

And may the Lord bless us,
and bless us kindly.

C.   *(From the Church in Kenya)*

From the cowardice
that does not face new truths,
from the laziness
that is content with half truths,

from the arrogance
that thinks it knows all the truth,
deliver us today, good Lord.

D.   *(From the Salvation Army)*

Lord, give to all those people
who have authority over others
the wisdom to govern well,
and the grace to know in their hearts
that nothing is firm which is not just,
and that the test of justice
is to turn people from following after evil
to seek what is good.

E.   *(From the Welsh Celtic tradition)*

Almighty Creator, maker of all things,
the world could not express your glory
even were the grass and the trees to sing.

You have made such a multitude of wonders
that they cannot be equalled.
No language can express them,
no letters can contain them.

Yet it is no hardship
to praise the Holy Trinity;
it is our delight
to praise the Son of Mary.

F.   *(From the Church in Nicaragua)*

Lord,
prevent us from falling into the sin
of believing that the slavery of Egypt
is better than the struggle in the desert.

G. *(From the Church in Sweden)*

Lord, we thank you
for all the light, grace and life
seen and known in the church which nurtured us.
Praying that, still may we be set free
from narrow-mindedness and complacency.

Open our eyes
that we may recognise the work of your Spirit
among other people and under different forms.

And should we yet walk in some things
on separate ways,
then present before us the common goal
towards which we travel.

H. *(From the Church in the Philippines)*

Lord, in these times,
when we fear we are losing hope
or feel that our efforts are futile,
let us see in our hearts and minds
the image of your resurrection,
and let that be our source of courage and strength.
With that, and in your company,
help us to face challenges and struggles
against all that is born of injustice.

I. *(From the Church in Hungary)*

Gather us or scatter us, O Lord,
according to your will.
Build us into one Church:
a Church with open doors and large windows,
a Church which takes the world seriously,
ready to work and to suffer,
and even to bleed for it.

J.   *(From the Church in Ghana)*

O Lord our God,
listening to us here,
you accept also the prayers
of our sisters and brothers
in Africa, Asia, the Pacific,
the Americas and Europe.

We are all one in prayer.
So may we, as one,
rightly carry out your commission
to witness and to love
in the church and throughout the world.
Accept our prayers graciously,
even when they are somewhat strange.
They are offered in Jesus' name.

K.   *(From the Scottish Celtic tradition)*

God, kindle within our hearts today
a flame of love for our neighbours,
for our foes,
for our friends,
for our people,
for the brave,
for the cowardly,
for the thoughtless ones.

O Son of the loveliest Mary,
in all that we love may we serve you,
from the lowliest thing that lives,
to the name that is highest of all.

L.   *(From unknown British source)*

O Christ, the Master Carpenter
who, at the last, through wood and nails,
purchased our whole salvation.
Wield well your tools
in the workshop of your world,
so that we,
who come rough-hewn to your bench,
may here be fashioned
to a truer beauty of your hand.
We ask it for your own name's sake.

Blessing

Leader: Lord, set your blessing on us
as we begin this day together.
Confirm in us the truth
by which we rightly live;
confront us with the truth
from which we wrongly turn.

We ask not for what we want
but for what you know we need,
as we offer this day and ourselves
for you and to you
through Jesus Christ, our Saviour
ALL: AMEN.

Leader: The Lord be with you.
ALL: AND ALSO WITH YOU.

Daytime liturgy A

Like DAYTIME LITURGY B, this liturgy is not limited to a particular time of day, and may be adapted for morning or evening use. It is based on Isaiah Chapter 35, one of the great passages of scripture in which God's will for justice for the world and its people is clearly stated.

During the PRAYERS OF CONCERN, which focus on daily bread for the world, there are pauses in which either the leader or members of the congregation may name specific individuals or causes.

Gathering song or silence

Call to worship

> *(From the back of worship area)*

Leader: All you who are thirsty,
this is the place for water.
All you who are hungry,
this is the place to be fed.

Why spend your earnings on what is not food?
Why pay for that which fails to satisfy?

Here, without money,
here, without price,
all may enjoy the bread of heaven.

God speaks,
and all who listen will have life.

Song or hymn   *(ALL standing)*

Prayer

Leader: Look for the Lord, while God is present;
          call out to God who is close at hand.

          (ALL sit)

          Let us pray.

          Glorious God,
          your thoughts are not our thoughts,
          nor are your ways our ways.

          You look at the ugliest soul
          and see, still unstirred,
          the wings of an angel.
ALL: WE SCAN THE FINEST OF OUR NEIGHBOURS,
          ANXIOUS TO FIND THE FLAWS.

Leader: You see our lives in the context of eternity,
          and make a time for waiting, for yearning,
          for putting all things in proportion.
ALL: WE DEMAND INSTANT RESULTS;
          AND LOOK FOR TOMORROW
          BEFORE SAVOURING TODAY.

Leader: You know that only one who suffers
          can ultimately save,
          so you choose to walk the way of the cross.
ALL: WE FEEL JUDGED AND THREATENED
          BY THAT LOVE WHICH RISKS ALL FOR ALL.

Leader: Your thoughts are not our thoughts,
ALL: NOR ARE YOUR WAYS OUR WAYS.

          (Pause)

Leader: Not to have our worst confirmed,
          but to have our best liberated,
          we pray for your grace and your pardon.

ALL: FORGIVE IN US WHAT HAS GONE WRONG,
          REPAIR IN US WHAT IS WASTED,
          REVEAL IN US WHAT IS GOOD.

Leader: And nourish us with better food
than we could ever purchase:
your Word,
your love
your interest,
your daily bread for our life's journey,
in the company of Jesus Christ our Lord.
ALL: AMEN.

Word of God

Reader: Listen for the Word of the Lord.
ALL: OUR EARS ARE OPEN.

Reader: We read from the book of ... chapter ... verse ...

(Scripture is read)

Reader: This is the Word/Gospel of the Lord;
ALL: THANKS BE TO GOD.

Prayers of concern

Leader: Let us pray.

Let us pray for those who hunger in this land:
whose only kitchen is a soup kitchen,
whose only food is what others don't want,
whose diet depends on luck, not on planning.

(Pause)

Lord, feed your people
using our skills and conscience,
and eradicate from our politics and private lives
the apathy to hunger which comes from over-eating.

Let us pray for the hungry and the fed.
ALL: LORD HAVE MERCY.

Leader: Let us pray for the hungry in other lands,
where economies, burdened by debt,
cannot respond to human need:
or where fields are farmed for our benefit
by low-waged workers courted by starvation.

(Pause)

Lord, feed your people,
even if rulers must cancel debt,
and shareholders lose profit,
or diners restrict their choice
in order that all may be nourished.

Let us pray for the hungry and the fed

ALL: LORD HAVE MERCY.

Leader: Let us pray for the hungry for justice,
who document inequalities,
demonstrate against tyranny,
distinguish between need and greed,
and are sometimes misrepresented or persecuted
in the process.

(Pause)

May their labour not be in vain
and may we be counted in their number.

Let us pray for the hungry and the fed.

ALL: LORD HAVE MERCY.

Leader: So, in the presence of the Bread of Life
who refused food for himself
in order to nourish others,
we deepen our devotion by praying his words:

ALL: OUR FATHER IN HEAVEN,
       HALLOWED BE YOUR NAME.
       YOUR KINGDOM COME,
       YOUR WILL BE DONE ON EARTH
       AS IN HEAVEN.
       GIVE US TODAY OUR DAILY BREAD.
       FORGIVE US OUR SINS
       AS WE FORGIVE THOSE WHO SIN AGAINST US.
       SAVE US FROM THE TIME OF TRIAL,
       AND DELIVER US FROM EVIL,
       FOR THE KINGDOM, THE POWER
       AND THE GLORY ARE YOURS,
       NOW AND FOR EVER.
       AMEN.

Song or hymn

Closing responses

Leader: Now may God
          who gives seed to the sower
          and corn to the reaper
          give to us all that is needed
          to produce a good harvest.
ALL: MAY GOD MAKE US FERTILE
          IN FAITH, LOVE AND GOODNESS,
          AND TAKE US OUT WITH JOY,
          AND LEAD US ON IN PEACE,
          AS SIGNS OF THE FRUITFULNESS OF HEAVEN.
          AMEN.

Daytime liturgy B

This liturgy is loosely based on the order for morning prayer in Iona Abbey. It allows for a specific time of corporate confession, and two optional opportunities for congregational participation.

With regard to the OPTIONAL BIBLICAL REFLECTION, if this is to be used, it is essential that the questions are open-ended and that in the larger gathering any sharing of people's insights are not 'capped' by the Leader, corrected or publicly refuted according to received theological wisdom.

With regard to the ALTERNATIVE PRAYER and lighting of candles, after the reading of scripture the congregation can be invited to remember people or situations which call for prayer. They may say a sentence about their intention, then light a small votive candle at the designated place. Note that there should be plentiful supplies of votive lights, larger candles from which to light them and tapers to aid this process.

Opening responses (ALL standing)

Leader:	The world belongs to the Lord,
ALL:	THE EARTH AND ALL ITS PEOPLE.
Leader:	How good and how lovely it is
ALL:	TO LIVE TOGETHER IN UNITY.
Leader:	Love and faith come together,
ALL:	JUSTICE AND PEACE JOIN HANDS.
Leader:	If the Lord's disciples keep silent,
ALL:	THESE STONES WOULD SHOUT ALOUD.
Leader:	Lord, open our lips
ALL:	AND OUR MOUTHS
	SHALL PROCLAIM YOUR PRAISE.

Psalm or song of praise

Prayer of confession *(ALL seated)*

Leader:	Holy God, Maker of all,
ALL:	HAVE MERCY ON US.
Leader:	Jesus Christ, Son of Mary,
ALL:	HAVE MERCY ON US.
Leader:	Holy Spirit, breath of life,
ALL:	HAVE MERCY ON US.

Leader: Let us in silence remember
our own faults and failings.

(Silence)

In the community of Christ's Church
and in the presence of all God's people,
I confess to God that I have sinned
in thought, word and deed.
I have not loved God, cared for God's world,
or respected God's people as I should.
I own my responsibility and pray for God's pardon.

ALL: MAY GOD FORGIVE YOU,
CHRIST BEFRIEND YOU,
AND THE SPIRIT RENEW
AND CHANGE YOUR LIFE.

Leader: Amen.

ALL: IN THE COMMUNITY OF CHRIST'S CHURCH
AND IN THE PRESENCE OF ALL GOD'S PEOPLE,
WE CONFESS TO GOD THAT WE HAVE SINNED
IN THOUGHT, WORD AND DEED.
WE HAVE NOT LOVED GOD,
CARED FOR GOD'S WORLD,
OR RESPECTED GOD'S PEOPLE AS WE SHOULD.
WE OWN OUR RESPONSIBILITY
AND PRAY FOR GOD'S PARDON.

Leader: May God forgive you,
Christ befriend you,
and the Spirit renew and change your life.

ALL: AMEN.

Leader: Turn again, O Lord, and give us life
ALL: THAT YOUR PEOPLE MAY REJOICE IN YOU.
Leader: Create in me a clean heart, O God,
ALL: AND RENEW A RIGHT SPIRIT WITHIN ME.
Leader: Give us again the joy of your help
ALL: WITH YOUR SPIRIT OF FREEDOM SUSTAIN US.

Leader: And now, as Jesus taught us, we say,

ALL: OUR FATHER IN HEAVEN,
            HALLOWED BE YOUR NAME,
            YOUR KINGDOM COME,
            YOUR WILL BE DONE ON EARTH
            AS IN HEAVEN.
            GIVE US TODAY OUR DAILY BREAD.
            FORGIVE US OUR SINS
            AS WE FORGIVE THOSE WHO SIN AGAINST US.
            SAVE US FROM THE TIME OF TRIAL
            AND DELIVER US FROM EVIL,
            FOR THE KINGDOM,
            THE POWER AND THE GLORY ARE YOURS,
            NOW AND FOR EVER.
            AMEN.

Word of God

Leader: Let us listen for the Word of the Lord
ALL: OUR EARS ARE OPEN.

            (Scripture is read)

Leader: Thanks be to God.
ALL: AMEN

Optional biblical reflection

            (The Leader may encourage people to reflect on the
            Bible passage in small groups by turning round to each
            other and discussing ONE of the following or a similar
            question:

1. Why, do you think, was this story included in the Bible?

2. What question does this passage lead us to ask God or each other?

3. Who or where in the world does this reading remind us of?

    After five minutes, the Leader may call everyone back together and ask if there is anything which people would like to share with the whole assembly)

Prayer

Leader: Eternal God,
            conceiver and shaper,
            ruler and saviour of the world,
            we bless you that, awake and aware,
            we are free to praise you.
            Bound in the family of Christ
            to worshippers in every land,
            we worship you in our mother tongue
            as others do in theirs,
            glad to be part of your pattern and purpose.
ALL: AMEN.

Leader: Liberate all who follow Christ
            from narrowness of vision
            and limited discipleship.
            Make your people keen to serve you
            in the public worlds of business,
            politics, education, law, industry
            and wherever the welfare of humanity
            may be improved or threatened.
            Thus may compassion and justice
            inform our national life and institutions
            as keenly as they address our consciences.
ALL: AMEN.

Leader: Throughout this day,
enliven our minds,
inspire our conversation,
inform our decisions,
and protect those we love.
And should today bring
what we neither anticipate nor desire,
increase our faith and decrease our pride
until we know that,
when we face the unexpected,
we do not stand alone.

Hear these prayers
made in the presence and in the name
of Jesus Christ our Lord.
ALL: AMEN.

Alternative prayer

*(If appropriate, the first two collects above may be
omitted and people can, if they wish, share with the
gathering a person or a cause they feel concerned
about, and light a small votive candle centrally as they
make their prayer.*

A pattern for these offerings might be:

I light this candle for N ... who is ... *[e.g. desperately
trying to come to terms with his addiction, etc.]*

or

I light this candle for the people of N ... who ...
[e.g. must be wondering if the world cares, etc.]

This activity can conclude with the third collect above)

Song or hymn *(ALL standing)*

Closing responses   *(ALL remain standing)*

Leader:	This is the day that the Lord has made.
ALL:	WE WILL REJOICE AND BE GLAD IN IT.
Leader:	We will not offer to God
ALL:	OFFERINGS THAT COST US NOTHING.
Leader:	Go in peace and serve the Lord.
ALL:	WE WILL SEEK PEACE AND PURSUE IT.

Leader:	Glory be to God who made us
	and to Christ who saved us
	and to the Holy Spirit who keeps us in faith,
ALL:	AS IT WAS IN THE BEGINNING,
	IS NOW,
	AND SHALL BE FOR EVER.
	AMEN.

Evening liturgy A

This simple order of evening prayer allows time for silent reflection throughout. Hymns and songs are optional, particularly if chants are to be used during the INVOCATION and PRAYERS OF CONCERN. It is important to have a large candle lit centrally for this liturgy and let the rest of the area be in subdued lighting.

Chant   *(Repeated after Cantor. See Appendix, page 114)*

COME, HOLY SPIRIT.
COME, HOLY SPIRIT.
MARANATHA!
COME, LORD, COME.

Invocation

Leader: Breath of God,
               breath of life,
               breath of deepest yearning,
ALL: COME, HOLY SPIRIT.   *(Spoken or sung as above)*

Leader: Comforter,
               Disturber,
               Interpreter,
               Enthuser,
ALL: COME, HOLY SPIRIT.

Leader: Heavenly Friend
               Lamplighter,
               Revealer of truth,
               Midwife of change,
ALL: COME, HOLY SPIRIT.

Leader: The Lord is here
ALL: GOD'S SPIRIT IS WITH US.

Song or hymn

(Optional and to be sung seated)

Prayer

Leader: Let us pray.

            Lord, teach us the silence of humility,
ALL: THE SILENCE OF WISDOM,
Leader: the silence of love,
ALL: THE SILENCE THAT SPEAKS WITHOUT WORDS,
Leader: the silence of faith.

ALL: LORD TEACH US
            TO SILENCE OUR OWN HEARTS AND MINDS
            THAT WE MAY LISTEN
            FOR THE MOVEMENT OF YOUR HOLY SPIRIT,
            AND FEEL YOUR PRESENCE
            IN THE DEPTHS OF OUR BEING.

Silence

Word of God

Reader: This is God's Word and it can be trusted.

            (A portion of scripture is read)

Reader: This is God's Word and it can be trusted.

Silence

Prayer of concern

*(During the PRAYERS, a chant such as LISTEN, LORD –
see Appendix, page 124 – may be sung to end the
silences following each bidding)*

Leader: Let us keep silence before God,
and through our minds and imaginations
offer prayers which words might not contain.

Let us pray.

There is a time for every purpose under heaven.

A time for gratitude ...

(Silence followed by chant as follows)

ALL: LISTEN LORD, LISTEN LORD,
NOT TO OUR WORDS BUT TO OUR PRAYER.
YOU ALONE, YOU ALONE
UNDERSTAND AND CARE.

Leader: A time for what we have to lay down ...

(Silence followed by chant)

Leader: A time for what we have to pick up ...

(Silence followed by chant)

Leader: A time for confronting what we are avoiding ...

(Silence followed by chant)

Leader: A time for recognising what we hope for ...

(Silence followed by chant)

Leader: In our time and in your time,
God fulfil our prayers
and let your kingdom come.
ALL: AMEN.

Song or hymn

Blessing

Leader: Now may the Spirit of God,
who brooded over the waters
and brought order out of chaos,
find a home in our hearts
and settle our minds as we sleep
that tomorrow we may wake
and live to God's glory.
ALL: AMEN.

Evening liturgy B

This liturgy presumes that people know or find out each other's names before worship begins. If the OPTIONAL MEDITATION is going to be used, everyone should be told in advance what happens, so that they can participate fully.

Opening responses   *(Seated or standing)*

Leader: Come, Lord Jesus,
               you too were tired
               when day was done;
               you met your friends at evening time.
ALL: COME, LORD JESUS.

Leader: Come, Lord Jesus,
               you too enjoyed
               when nights drew on;
               you told your tales at close of day.
ALL: COME, LORD JESUS.

Leader: Come, Lord Jesus,
               you kindled faith
               when lamps were low;
               you opened scriptures,
               broke the bread,
               and shed your light
               as darkness fell.
ALL: COME, LORD JESUS,
               MEET US HERE.

Song or hymn   *(Seated or standing)*

Prayer   *(ALL sit)*

Leader: Let us pray.

You broke down the barriers
when you crept in beside us.
For in Jesus ... the smiling Jesus,
the story-telling Jesus,
the controversial Jesus,
the annoying Jesus,
the loving and forgiving Jesus,
your hands touched all, and touched us,
showing how in Christ
there is neither Jew nor Gentile,
neither male nor female:

ALL: ALL ARE ONE IN JESUS CHRIST
AND FOR THIS WE PRAISE YOU.

Leader: You opened our eyes,
to see how the hands of the rich were empty
and the hearts of the poor were full.
You dared to take the widow's mite,
the child's loaves,
the babe at the breast,
and in these simple things
to point out the path to your Kingdom.
You said, 'Follow me!',
for on our own we could never discover
that in Christ
there is neither Jew nor Gentile,
neither male nor female:

ALL: ALL ARE ONE IN JESUS CHRIST
AND FOR THIS WE PRAISE YOU.

Leader: You gave us hands to hold:
black hands and white hands,
African hands and Asian hands,
the clasping hands of lovers,
and the reluctant hands of those
who don't believe they are worth holding.
And when we wanted to shake our fist,
you still wanted to hold our hand,
because in Christ
there is neither Jew nor Gentile,
neither male nor female:

ALL: ALL ARE ONE IN JESUS CHRIST
AND FOR THIS WE PRAISE YOU.

Leader: Here in the company
             of the neighbour whom we know
             and the stranger in our midst,
             and the self from whom we turn,
             we ask to love as Jesus loved.
             Make this the place and time, good Lord,
             when heaven and earth merge into one,
             and we in word and flesh can grasp
             that in Christ
             there is neither Jew nor Gentile,
                      neither male nor female:
ALL: ALL ARE ONE IN JESUS CHRIST,
             AND FOR THIS WE PRAISE YOU.
             AMEN.

Word of God

             (Either a portion of scripture may be read, ending with:

Reader: This is the Gospel/Word of the Lord
ALL: THANKS BE TO GOD.

             or

             *the Leader may invite people to close their eyes and,
             from memory, to recall what – for them – are significant
             Gospel pictures of Jesus. The Leader may begin with the
             following example, then others can follow the pattern,
             beginning with the phrase, 'I see Jesus ... ':*

Leader: I see Jesus ...
             sitting in a boat looking at the crowds of people
             who have come to hear him.

             *It may be helpful to sing the chant BEHOLD THE LAMB
             OF GOD – see Appendix, page 113 – before and after
             each remembrance. The Leader may end the meditation
             by saying:)*

Leader: Thanks be to God who has met us in Jesus.
ALL: AMEN.

Song or hymn

(Optional, but recommended if MEDITATION has been used)

Prayers

(After each category, anyone may offer a name or short prayer for those brought to mind. Each can be followed by a said or sung response, such as:

Cantor: Lord, draw near,
ALL: LORD. DRAW NEAR,
DRAW NEAR, DRAW NEAR AND STAY.

or

Cantor: Lord, in your mercy,
ALL: HEAR OUR PRAYER.*)*

Leader: Let us say a prayer for those who need to be remembered tonight:

Those who have made the news headlines today because of what they have done or said ...

Those who have been brought to our attention through a meeting or conversation ...

Those who are in hospital, in care, or in a place which is strange to them ...

Those in whose family, marriage or close relationship, there is stress or a break-up ...

Those who are waiting for a birth, or a death, or news which will affect their lives ...

Those who need to forget
the God they do not believe in
and meet the God who believes in them ...

Those whose pain or potential
we should not forget to share with God tonight ...

Lord, we believe that you hear our prayer
and will be faithful to your promise to answer us.

When our eyes open again,
may they do so
not to end our devotions,
but to expect your kingdom,
for Jesus' sake.

ALL: AMEN.

Song or hymn   *(Seated or standing)*

Blessing

*(Before the written BLESSING, people may wish to join
hands and say thank you to God for each other. The
Leader begins by saying: 'Thank you, God, for N ...'
[person on his/her left], then that person prays for the
person to his/her left and so on round the circle)*

Leader: May God bless us
in our sleep with rest,
in our dreams with vision,
in our waking with a calm mind,
in our soul with the friendship of the Holy Spirit
this night and every night.

ALL: AMEN.

Evening liturgy C

*Like MORNING LITURGY D, this has been shaped from original
material gathered in the Scottish Highlands and Islands. The PRAYER is
simple and direct and should not be hurried. For the OPENING
RESPONSES, three people should each have a sizeable candle which
they light and place in an agreed and visible central location.*

Opening responses   *(Seated)*

Leader 1:   I will light a light
         in the name of the Maker,
         who lit the world
         and breathed the breath of life for me.

ALL: *(THE IONA GLORIA – see Appendix, page 115 – may
         be sung as a candle is lit and placed centrally)*

Leader 2:   I will light a light
         in the name of the Son,
         who saved the world
         and stretched out his hand to me.

ALL: *(THE IONA GLORIA may be sung as before, as a
         candle is lit and placed centrally)*

Leader 3:   I will light a light
         in the name of the Spirit,
         who encompasses the world
         and blessed my soul with yearning.

ALL: *(THE IONA GLORIA may be sung as before, as a
         candle is lit and placed centrally)*

ALL:
WE WILL LIGHT THREE LIGHTS
FOR THE TRINITY OF LOVE:
GOD ABOVE US,
GOD BESIDE US,
GOD BENEATH US;
THE BEGINNING,
THE END,
THE EVERLASTING ONE.

Song or hymn *(Seated or standing)*

Prayer   *(ALL sit)*

Leader: The knees of our hearts we bow
ALL: IN THE SIGHT OF GOD WHO CREATED US,
IN THE SIGHT OF THE SON WHO DIED FOR US,
IN THE SIGHT OF THE SPIRIT WHO HELPS US,
IN FRIENDSHIP AND AFFECTION.

Leader: Through your own son, O Maker of all,
grant us the fullness our lives long for:
ALL: LOVE FOR GOD,
LOVE FROM GOD,
THE SMILE OF GOD,
THE GRACE OF GOD,
THE WISDOM OF GOD,
THE FEAR OF GOD,
THE IMAGINATION OF GOD,
AND GOD'S PURPOSE IN ALL THINGS.

Leader: So may we live in this world
as saints and angels do in heaven.
ALL: EACH SHADOW AND LIGHT,
EACH DAY AND NIGHT,
EACH MOMENT IN KINDNESS,
GIVE US YOUR SPIRIT.
AMEN.

Word of God

Leader: O God of the weak,
O God of the lowly,
O God of the righteous,
O shield of your people,
ALL: SPEAK NOW THROUGH YOUR WORD.

Reader: *(A portion of scripture is read clearly, followed by a brief silence)*

Evening prayers

(Prayers may be said for others ad lib. Each prayer may end with the following call and response:

Prayer: Lord, hear my prayer
ALL: AT THE THRONE OF THE KING OF HEAVEN.

The prayer may be ended by the following:)

Leader: O God of all gods,
grant us your light this night,
your grace as we sleep,
your joy in the morning
and let us be made pure in the well of your health.
ALL: LIFT FROM US ANY ANGUISH,
TAKE FROM US EMPTY PRIDE,
AND LIGHTEN OUR SOULS
WITH THE LIGHT OF YOUR LOVE.

Leader: Jesus Christ, Son of Mary,
Holy Spirit, Light of Life,
shield and sustain us
and all our dear ones,
this night and every night.
ALL: AMEN.

Blessing

Leader:	On our heads and our houses,
ALL:	THE BLESSING OF GOD.
Leader:	In our coming and going,
ALL:	THE PEACE OF GOD.
Leader:	In our life and believing,
ALL:	THE LOVE OF GOD.
Leader:	At our end and new beginning,
ALL:	THE ARMS OF GOD TO WELCOME US AND BRING US HOME. AMEN.

Evening liturgy D

Caring for the earth has not been a predominant feature of Christian witness. Even today, when environmentalists warn of global disaster due to the demands on finite resources of western lifestyles, some churches are wary of taking up the challenge, lest they be dubbed 'New Age'. Caring for the earth is an imperative deeply rooted in the Bible, not least because it was for and into the material universe Christ came, to redeem the whole world, not just its human inhabitants.

If any of the OPTIONAL SYMBOLIC ACTIONS are being used, it is worth spending some time setting up the worship environment with an eye to the practicalities of space, sight-lines and movement from the congregation's point of view.

Opening acclamation

> (ALL stand. The DUNCAN ALLELUIA or the PERUVIAN GLORIA – see Appendix for both, pages 112 & 116 – are appropriate to sing between each section)

Leader: Beneath the mists of time,
            before the world began,
            beyond our understanding:
            in the beginning ... God.

ALL: (ALLELUIA or GLORIA or other chant may be sung)

Leader: Fathering history,
            mothering creation,
            parenting earth's people
            from the beginning ... God.

ALL: (ALLELUIA or GLORIA as above)

Leader: Expecting the right moment,
            preparing the right way,
            revealing the right person
            for each new beginning ... God.

ALL: *(ALLELUIA or GLORIA as above)*

Leader: We believe in one God,
ALL: MAKER AND MOVER OF HEAVEN AND EARTH.

Song or hymn

Prayer *(ALL sitting)*

Leader: Let us pray.

     God,
     God the Maker,
     maker of colour, sound, texture, quietness,
     and the restless beauty in living things,
ALL: WE BLESS YOU.

Leader: God,
     God the Maker,
     maker of granite and mustard seed,
      of grey cloud and starlight,
      of earthquake and heartbeat,
ALL: WE BLESS YOU.

Leader: God,
     God the Maker,
     maker of all that is unseen,
      of all that has been,
      of all that words could never capture,
ALL: WE BLESS YOU.

Leader: God,
     God our Maker,
     we, the children of your love,
      the creatures of your kindness,
      the guardians of your creation,
     bless you.

ALL: WE BLESS YOU FOR YOUR MAKING,
YOUR TRUSTING,
YOUR LOVING,
YOUR NEVER-ENDING GOODNESS.
AMEN.

Psalm 8 *(ALL standing)*

Leader: O Lord our God,
how glorious is your name in all the earth;
your majesty is praised above the heavens.
ALL: ON THE LIPS OF CHILDREN AND BABIES
YOU HAVE FOUND PRAISE
TO FOIL YOUR ENEMY,
TO SILENCE THE FOE AND THE REBEL.

Leader: When I look at the heavens,
the work of your hands,
at the moon and stars which you arranged,
what are human beings
that you should remember them,
mere mortals
that you should care for them?

Women: You have made them in your own image,
and crowned them with glory and honour;
Men: you have given them responsibility
for your handwork,
and put all things under their dominion;
Leader: all of them, sheep and cattle,
yes, even the savage beasts,
birds of the air and fish
that make their way through the waters.

ALL: O LORD, OUR GOD,
HOW GLORIOUS IS YOUR NAME
IN ALL THE EARTH!

(ALL sit)

Word of God

Reader: Listen for the Word of the Lord;
ALL: OUR EARS ARE OPEN.

     (A passage of scripture is read)

Reader: This is the Word/Gospel of the Lord.
ALL: THANKS BE TO GOD.

Optional reflection

     (The Leader may ask people to discuss the following
     question:)

Leader: If this is the Word of God
     which is meant to change our lives,
     how will our lives change in the next few days,
     having heard it?

     (The passage may be read again. Then people can be
     invited to turn to each other in small groups to discuss
     their response. After five minutes, the conversations can
     be brought to a close by singing the chant used at the
     beginning – which people will know – or by the
     introduction to the next song being played or hummed
     through.)

Song or hymn

Prayers

     (The PRAYERS may be said as indicated below, or one
     of the suggested SYMBOLIC ACTIONS may be
     substituted, followed by the Leader saying the final
     collect on page 73)

Leader: Let us pray for God's world.

That its beauty may be preserved,
　　its variety retained,
　　its integrity respected,
ALL: LORD, HEAR US.

Leader: That pollution and cruel exploitation might cease
so that rivers can clap their hands,
　　waste places burst into flower,
　　valleys laugh and sing,
　　wild life live in safety,
and all as you intended,
ALL: LORD, HEAR US.

Leader: That the children of tomorrow
may not need a museum to show them
the wonders of nature today,
ALL: LORD, HEAR US.

Leader: That the poorest nations of the world
may not harvest their fields
only to fill foreign tables,
ALL: LORD, HEAR US.

Leader: That Christ who pointed to the birds,
the flowers, the corn, the sunset,
might not find their beauty lacking
were he to return.
ALL: LORD, HEAR US.

Leader: Hear us, Creator of all;
convert the hearts of those who ravage the earth,
and strengthen the resolve of those who respect it.
And since the earth is your gift to us,
prevent us from destroying by thoughtlessness
that which is not ours to own.
ALL: AMEN.

Optional symbolic actions

*(One of these may be used as an alternative to the
PRAYER above.*

1. *A large map of the world may be placed in the centre
   of the worship area before the liturgy begins, with a
   number of small votive candles in baskets at its corners,
   and a larger lit candle in the middle.*

   *People may be invited to light a small votive candle and
   place it on the appropriate part of the map for which
   they have a particular concern. This best happens as
   music is played or a chant is sung.*

2. *A display of pictures or magazine cuttings depicting the
   beauty of the earth and its despoliation may be
   assembled round the periphery of the worship area.
   Then, as quiet music begins to play, the Leader may
   invite people to visit these areas and reflect on what
   they see.*

   The following introduction can be used:

Leader: Let us do as Jesus said ...
consider the lilies of the field,
think of the birds of the air ...
and as we do so, pray for the welfare of the world.

3. *Some people should be designated in advance to collect
   interesting natural objects, e.g. multicoloured autumn
   leaves or cones; washed stones and pebbles; bleached
   sticks from the sea shore; a clear glass bowl of water;
   bird feathers; flowers; beeswax/honeycomb.*

   *Using the same or comparable introductory words, the
   Leader may initiate a time of seated reflection. As music
   is played quietly, these objects may be passed round and
   eventually placed on a central table around a cross or
   candle.*

   *The closing collect on page 73 should follow any
   SYMBOLIC ACTION.)*

Song or hymn

Closing responses

Leader: Bless to us, O God,
ALL: THE MOON THAT IS ABOVE US,
THE EARTH THAT IS BENEATH US,
THE FRIENDS WHO ARE AROUND US,
YOUR IMAGE DEEP WITHIN US,
THE REST WHICH IS BEFORE US.
AMEN.

Evening liturgy E

This liturgy celebrates the worshipping life of the Church and prays for its renewal. If the OPTIONAL CONVERSATION is going to take place, it may be sensitive to mention this in advance, so people feel at ease with it. It is also important that in the PRAYERS OF CONCERN, different people should read the petitions and do so from different places in the worship area.

Opening responses   *(ALL standing)*

Leader:	We are met in the presence of God,
ALL:	AND WE DO NOT MEET ALONE.

Leader:	With the angels in highest heaven,
ALL:	WE GATHER TO WORSHIP THE LORD.
Leader:	With the saints of every age,
ALL:	WE GATHER TO WORSHIP THE LORD.
Leader:	With the Church throughout the world,
ALL:	WE GATHER TO WORSHIP THE LORD.

Leader:	By children and babes at the breast,
ALL:	GOD'S HOLY NAME IS PRAISED.
Leader:	With drums, sitars and trumpets,
ALL:	GOD'S HOLY NAME IS PRAISED.
Leader:	In barrios and basilicas,
ALL:	GOD'S HOLY NAME IS PRAISED.
Leader:	And here with our hearts and our voices,
ALL:	GOD'S HOLY NAME IS PRAISED.

Leader:	We are met in the presence of God,
ALL:	AND WE DO NOT MEET ALONE.

Psalm or hymn of praise

Prayer   *(ALL seated)*

Leader: Let us pray.

Generous God, you gave us our voices,
no two the same,
no finer instruments with which to praise you.

ALL: FOR THESE WE THANK YOU, LORD.

Leader: You gave us words and music,
peculiar gifts,
with which to wound or wonder,
bore or bless, inspire or disable.

ALL: FOR THESE WE THANK YOU, LORD.

Leader: And in your Church you have gathered us.
In your community
of common folk and complainers,
prophets and puzzled people,
you have made a place for us.

ALL: FOR THIS WE THANK YOU, LORD.

Leader: So let what we say and do here,
what we ponder and decide here,
be real for us and honest to you,
and prepare us for the life of the world
in which you are also praised.

ALL: AMEN.

Psalm 146   *(ALL standing)*

Reader: Sing praise to the Lord who is good,
sing to our God who is loving:

ALL: TO GOD ALL PRAISE IS DUE.

Reader: The Lord builds up Jerusalem
and brings back Israel's exiles;

Women: God heals the broken-hearted,
and binds up all their wounds.

Men: God fixes the number of the stars
and calls each one by its name.

Reader:	The Lord is great and all-knowing;
	God's wisdom can never be measured.
Women:	The Lord raises the lowly,
	and humbles the wicked to the dust.
Men:	O sing to the Lord, giving thanks,
	sing psalms to our God with the harp.

Reader:	God covers the earth with clouds
	and prepares rain for the earth;
Women:	God clothes the mountains with grass
	and with plants to serve human needs;
Men:	God provides the beasts with their food,
	and tends to the young ravens' cry.

Reader:	God takes no delight in weapons,
	nor pleasure in warriors' strength,
ALL:	GOD DELIGHTS
	IN THOSE WHO SHOW REVERENCE,
	IN THOSE WHO TRUST IN GOD'S LOVE.

Song

(An ALLELUIA, such as the DUNCAN ALLELUIA – see Appendix, page 112 – may be sung and people stand or sit for the WORD OF GOD according to local custom. If appropriate, the ALLELUIA may be sung again after the reading)

Word of God

Reader:	We read in the book of ... chapter ... at verse ... to ...
	Hear the Word of God,
ALL:	OUR EARS ARE OPEN.

(Scripture is read)

| Leader: | This is the Word of the Lord. |
| ALL: | THANKS BE TO GOD. |

Optional conversation

(If appropriate, people may now be engaged in a conversation with regard to the worship of the Church. Any one of these sample questions or others like them may initiate group conversation. These may be brought to a close with the singing of the ALLELUIA again, or some music played quietly)

1. If Jesus were to come to the church we go to on Sunday, where would he sit or whom would he sit beside and why?

2. If Jesus were in our church on Sunday, and in the spirit of the Book of Revelation he were to address a word to the community, what, in a sentence, do you think he would say?

3. *(In conjunction with the reading, which might have to be read again after this question is asked)*

    If, as in Luke's Gospel, Jesus had stood up to read the Bible portion we just heard, and then sat down to speak about it, what do you think he would have highlighted?

Prayers of concern

(People may be invited to say the first names aloud of people they wish to pray for at the end of each section. After names have been said, a chant such as JESUS CHRIST, SON OF GOD AMONG US – see Appendix, page 122 – may be sung. Note there is no chant after section D)

Leader A: Eternal God,
whom our words may cradle but never contain,
we thank you for all the sound and silence
and colour and symbol
which through the centuries have helped
the worship of your Church
to be relevant and real.

Here we pause to remember those
who helped us to come to faith,
by singing us songs or telling us stories,
by inviting us in when we felt distant,
by praying for us without being asked.

We name them now.

(Names are mentioned, followed by the chant)

Leader B: We remember the preachers, the readers,
the musicians, the leaders,
whose sensitivity and skill
have helped us to grow in faith
and enjoy worshipping you.

We name them now.

(Names are mentioned, followed by the chant)

Leader C: We remember those
who encourage people to praise you
outside the sanctuary:
– those who teach young children,
– those who lead youth groups,
– those who take prayers in hospitals,
in schools,
in prisons.
And we name them now.

(Names are mentioned, followed by the chant)

Leader D: We remember people who cannot pray
and struggle to believe,
or who fear changes in the church
more than in any other area of their lives.

We name them now,
praying that they might be encouraged,
and that love might dispel fear.

(Names are mentioned. No chant is sung)

Leader A: And let us pray for the renewal of the Church,
beginning with ourselves.

ALL: RESHAPE US, GOOD LORD,
UNTIL IN GENEROSITY,
IN FAITH,
AND IN EXPECTATION
THAT THE BEST IS YET TO COME,
WE ARE TRULY CHRIST-LIKE.

MAKE US PASSIONATE FOLLOWERS OF JESUS
RATHER THAN PASSIVE SUPPORTERS.

MAKE OUR CHURCHES
CELLS OF RADICAL DISCIPLESHIP
AND SIGNPOSTS TO HEAVEN,
THEN, IN US, THROUGH US,
AND – IF NEED BE – DESPITE US,
LET YOUR KINGDOM COME.
AMEN.

Song or hymn

Closing responses

Leader: From where we are
to where you need us,
ALL: CHRIST BE BESIDE US.

Leader: From what we are
to what you can make of us,
ALL: CHRIST BE BEFORE US.

Leader: From the mouthing of generalities
to making signs of your kingdom,
ALL: CHRIST BE BENEATH US.

Leader: Through the streets of this world
to the gates of heaven,
ALL: CHRIST BE ABOVE US.

Leader: Surround us with your presence,
inspire us with your purpose,
confirm us in your love.
ALL: AMEN.

Liturgy for Holy Communion A

This is the longer of the two orders for Communion. It has more formal language and presumes a church or large assembly setting.

There is a choice of CALL TO WORSHIP and there is an alternative Eucharistic prayer for festivals (FESTIVAL PREFACE, see suggestions on page 90) as well as a range of seasonal Eucharistic sentences for use prior to the reception of the bread and wine (ALTERNATIVE SENTENCES). These are given at the end of the liturgy. In the PRAYER OF ADORATION, mention is made of saints appropriate to the denomination or occasion. These should be changed or substituted ad lib.

Following one historical British tradition, THE STORY (the scriptural narrative or warrant) is read before the EUCHARISTIC PRAYER; and the PEACE is passed after Communion, thus heightening the sense of the sacrament as a means of grace.

For a musical setting of the SANCTUS and BENEDICTUS, see the Appendix, page 126.

Gathering song or silence

(One of the following two CALLS TO WORSHIP may be used)

Call to worship I   *(ALL standing)*

Leader: Gather us in,
             the lost and the lonely,
             the broken and breaking,
             the tired and the aching
             who long for the nourishment
             found at your feast.

80

ALL: GATHER US IN,
Leader: the done and the doubting,
           the wishing and wondering,
           the puzzled and pondering
           who long for the company
           found at your feast.

ALL: GATHER US IN,
Leader: the proud and pretentious,
           the sure and superior,
           the never inferior,
           who long for the levelling
           found at your feast.

ALL: GATHER US IN,
Leader: the bright and the bustling,
           the stirrers, the shakers,
           the kind laughter makers
           who long for the deeper joys
           found at your feast.

ALL: GATHER US IN,
Leader: from corner or limelight,
           from mansion or campsite,
           from fears and obsession,
           from tears and depression,
           from untold excesses,
           from treasured successes,
           to meet, to eat,
           be given a seat,
           be joined to the vine,
           be offered new wine,
           become like the least,
           be found at the feast.

ALL: GATHER US IN!

           or

Call to worship 2

Leader: We meet in the name of God,
    Creator of the universe,
    source of true humanity,
    mother and father of all.
ALL: AMEN. *(Spoken or sung)*

Leader: We meet in the name of Jesus,
    Word made flesh,
    saviour of fallen humanity,
    lover of all.
ALL: AMEN. *(As above)*

Leader: We meet in the name of the Holy Spirit,
    Lord and giver of life,
    midwife of new humanity,
    inspirer of all.
ALL: AMEN. *(As above)*

Leader: Come then, eternal God
ALL: BE PRESENT HERE,
    BEFRIEND US HERE,
    RENEW US HERE.

Song or hymn

(ALL sit)

Prayer of adoration

(Change saints' names as appropriate*)

Leader: Heaven is here, and earth,
    and the space is thin between them.
    Distance may divide,
    but Christ's promise unites
    those bounded by time,
    those blessed by eternity.

| | Let heaven be glad; |
| *ALL:* | LET THE WHOLE EARTH CRY GLORY. |

Leader: Heaven is here, and earth,
and the Church above and below is one.
Peter is here, and Paul,
Martha and all the Marys,
Columba and Francis, Theresa and Luther King; *
the saints from far back
and those who left us not long ago.
And only sight prevents us
from seeing them,
one with us on the other side.
Let heaven be glad,

ALL: LET THE WHOLE EARTH CRY GLORY.

Leader: Heaven is here, and earth,
and the God who made them is present.
The Lamb, glorious on the throne,
sits beside us;
the Spirit of God, the Dove,
makes her resting place among us.

God inhales the breath of our prayers
and spreads a table for our satisfaction.

Let heaven be glad,

ALL: LET THE WHOLE EARTH CRY GLORY.

Leader: Blessing and honour and glory and power
be to our God for ever and ever.

ALL: AMEN.

Scripture

Song or chant

Invitation   *(Optional)*

Celebrant: He was always the guest.

In the homes of Peter and Jairus,
Martha and Mary, Joanna and Susanna,
he was always the guest.

At the meal tables of the wealthy
where he pled the case of the poor,
he was always the guest.

Upsetting polite company,
befriending isolated people,
welcoming the stranger,
he was always the guest.

But here,
at this table,
he is the host.

Those who wish to serve him
must first be served by him,
those who want to follow him
must first be fed by him,
those who would wash his feet
must first let him make them clean.

For this is the table
where God intends us to be nourished;
this is the time
when Christ can make us new.

So come, you who hunger and thirst
for a deeper faith,
for a better life,
for a fairer world.

Jesus Christ,
who has sat at our tables,
now invites us to be guests at his.

Song

(During which bread and wine may be brought forward/ into the gathering)

The story

Celebrant: What we do here, we do
in imitation of what Christ first did.

To his followers in every age,
Jesus gave an example and command
rooted in the experience he shared
with his disciples
in an upstairs room in Jerusalem.

Reader: On the night on which he was betrayed,
and as they were sitting at a meal,
Jesus took a piece of bread and broke it.
He gave it to the disciples saying,
'This is my body. It is broken for you.
Do this to remember me.'

Later, after they had eaten,
he took a cup of wine and said,
'This cup is the new relationship with God
made possible because of my death.
Drink this all of you, to remember me.'

Celebrant: So now we do as Jesus did.

We take this bread and this wine,
the produce of the earth and fruit of human labour.

In these, Jesus has promised to be present;
through these, Christ can make us whole.

Eucharistic prayer

Celebrant: Let us pray.

                The Lord be with you.
ALL: AND ALSO WITH YOU.

Celebrant: Lift up your hearts.
ALL: WE LIFT THEM TO THE LORD.

Celebrant: Let us give thanks to the Lord our God.
ALL: IT IS RIGHT TO GIVE OUR THANKS AND PRAISE.

                (For ALTERNATIVE FESTIVAL PREFACE, see page 90)

Celebrant: It is indeed right,
                for you made us,
                and before us, you made the world we inhabit,
                and before the world, you made the eternal home
                in which, through Christ, we have a place.

                All that is spectacular,
                all that is plain
                have their origin in you;
                all that is lovely,
                all who are loving
                point to you as their fulfilment.

                And grateful as we are
                for the world we know
                and the universe beyond our ken,
                we particularly praise you,
                whom eternity cannot contain,
                for coming to earth and entering time
                in Jesus.

                For his life which informs our living,
                for his compassion which changes our hearts,
                for his clear speaking
                which contradicts our harmless generalities,
                for his disturbing presence,
                    his innocent suffering,

his fearless dying,
his rising to life breathing forgiveness,
we praise you and worship him.

Here too our gratitude rises
for the promise of the Holy Spirit,
who even yet, even now,
confronts us with your claims
and attracts us to your goodness.

Therefore we gladly join our voices
to the song of the Church
on earth and in heaven:

Sanctus: HOLY, HOLY, HOLY LORD,
GOD OF POWER AND MIGHT.
HEAVEN AND EARTH ARE FULL OF YOUR GLORY.
HOSANNA IN THE HIGHEST.

Benedictus: BLESSED IS HE WHO COMES
IN THE NAME OF THE LORD.
HOSANNA IN THE HIGHEST.

Celebrant: And now,
lest we believe
that our praise alone fulfils your purpose,
we fall silent
and remember him who came
because words weren't enough.

Setting our wisdom,
    our will,
        our words aside,
emptying our hearts,
and bringing nothing in our hands,
we yearn for the healing,
            the holding,
            the accepting,
            the forgiving
which Christ alone can offer.

(Silence)

Merciful God,
send now,
in kindness,
your Holy Spirit to settle on this bread and wine
and fill them with the fullness of Jesus.

And let that same Spirit rest on us,
converting us
from the patterns of this passing world,
until we conform to the shape of him
whose food we now share.
Amen.

Fraction   *(Taking and breaking bread)*

Celebrant: Among friends, gathered round a table,
Jesus took bread, and broke it, and said,
'This is my body – broken for you.'

(Holding up a cup of wine)

Later he took a cup of wine and said,
'This is the new relationship with God
made possible because of my death.
Take it, all of you, to remember me.'

Jesus, firstborn of Mary,
ALL: HAVE MERCY ON US

Celebrant: Jesus, Saviour of the world,
ALL: HAVE MERCY ON US.

Celebrant: Jesus, monarch of heaven,
ALL: GRANT US PEACE.

(For ALTERNATIVE SENTENCES, see page 91)

Celebrant: He whom the universe could not contain,
is present to us in this bread.
He who redeemed us and called us by name
now meets us in this cup.

So take this bread and this wine.
In them God comes to us
so that we may come to God.

(The sharing of the bread and wine)

The Peace

Celebrant: Please stand.

Christ who has nourished us,
is our peace.
Strangers and friends, male and female,
old and young,
he has broken down the barriers
to bind us to him
and to each other.

Having tasted his goodness,
let us share his peace.

The peace of the Lord be always with you.
ALL: AND ALSO WITH YOU.

(The PEACE is shared)

Concluding prayer

Leader: Let us pray.

In gratitude, in deep gratitude
for this moment,
    this meal,
    these people,
we give ourselves to you.

Take us out
to live as changed people
because we have shared the Living Bread
and cannot remain the same.

Ask much of us,
expect much from us,
enable much by us,
encourage many through us.

So. Lord, may we live to your glory,
both as inhabitants of earth
and citizens of the commonwealth of heaven.
Amen.

Closing song

Closing responses

Leader: Christ's food in our souls,
ALL: OUR FOOD SHARED LIKE HIS.
Leader: Christ's life in our hands,
ALL: OUR LIVES SHAPED BY HIS.
Leader: Christ's love in our hearts,
ALL: OUR LOVE WARMED THROUGH HIS.
Leader: Christ's peace on our path,
ALL: OUR PATH FOLLOWING HIS.

Benediction *(Optional)*

Recessional

Festival preface

Celebrant: Since you have called us,
since you have kept a place for us,
since your face lights up when we sit at your table,
gracious God,
ALL: HOW CAN WE KEEP FROM SINGING?

Celebrant: When deep down ... despite the contradictions,
              we know,
              we sense,
              we believe that life is good;
              when one of your words
              rings truer than ever before,
              when in one unexpected moment
              we are given a glimpse of your kingdom,
              gracious God,
ALL: HOW CAN WE KEEP FROM SINGING?

Celebrant: In this place
              where prayer has been made for many years,
              in this place
              where so many different people have found
              their common bond in your call and purpose,
              in this place
              where the walls are waiting
              to echo your praise,
              gracious God,
ALL: HOW CAN WE KEEP FROM SINGING?

Celebrant: Therefore with the Church throughout the world,
                        with the Church on the other side of time,
                            with those who once praised you here
              and have now joined the closer harmony of heaven,
              we sing the song of your everlasting praise:

ALL: (The SANCTUS is sung)

Alternative sentences

Advent

              He who was with God in the beginning,
              is with us in this bread.
              He of whom the prophets spoke,
              now speaks to us in this cup.

Christmas & Epiphany

> He who was first held by Mary
> is held for us in this bread.
> He whose body was laid in a manger,
> is cradled in this cup.

Lent

> He who has suffered for our injustices
> is now present in this bread.
> He whose body was hung on a cross,
> is now offered to us in this cup.

Easter

> He who was buried but rose from the dead
> is now present in this bread.
> He whose wounded hands
> were offered to the unbelieving,
> now reaches out in this cup.

Pentecost

> He who breathed on his first disciples,
> is present for us in this bread.
> He whose Spirit stirred the Church at Pentecost,
> now revives us in this cup.

Marriage

> He whose company once cheered a wedding feast,
> now is present in this bread.
> He whose word turned water into wine,
> now refreshes us in this cup.

Funeral

> He who grieved for the death of his friend,
> shares his solidarity through this bread.
> He who is surrounded by the saints in high heaven,
> offers his consolation in this cup.

Liturgy for Holy Communion B

This is the shorter of the two Communion liturgies. If need be, it may be advertised as either A SHORTER ORDER or A SHORTER CELEBRATION OF HOLY COMMUNION, never 'An Informal Communion'.

The original setting for this liturgy was a sitting room. It therefore presumes an intimacy of place and people.

Preparatory reading

> *(If appropriate, one of the following scripture passages may be read after people have gathered round a bare table. As the words are read slowly, a cloth may be spread, candles lit and any relevant symbols placed on or near the table.*
>
> *Biblical passages:*
> Psalm 23   *– The Lord is my Shepherd*
> Isaiah 25: 6–9   *– A Banquet of Rich Fare*
> Luke 14: 15–24   *– The Great Feast*
> Luke 24: 13–31   *– The Emmaus Road)*

Opening sentences

Leader: As if this were the only time,
and this the only place,
and we the only people,
Jesus Christ will meet us.

As if this were the only time,
and this the only place,
and we the only people,
let us worship God.

Song of praise

Prayer

Leader: You found out what we were doing
and you intervened.
'Come and do it together,
come and do it with me,' you said.

ALL: SO, THANK YOU, LORD,
FOR INTERVENING IN OUR PRIVATE LIVES.

Leader: You promised us nothing
by way of success, recognition,
possessions or reward.
'These things will come at the right time
when you walk with me,' you said.

ALL: SO, THANK YOU, LORD,
FOR PROMISING US NOTHING.

Leader: You gave us no resources apart from ourselves –
hands meant for caring,
lips meant for praising,
hearts meant for loving –
and the Holy Spirit to make us restless
until we change.

ALL: SO, THANK YOU, LORD,
FOR THE ESSENTIAL GIFTS.

Leader: Then just when we think we've got it right
as to where we should go and what we should do;
just when we're ready to take on the world,
you come, like a beggar, to our back door,
saying, 'This is the way.
I am the way.'
And offering us bread and wine.

ALL: SO, THANK YOU, LORD,
FOR COMING AGAIN
AND KEEPING YOUR WORD,
AND SHOWING YOU CARE
FOR US AND FOR ALL PEOPLE.
AMEN.

Word of God

(Either a member of the gathering may read an appropriate scripture passage or: the Leader may invite people to close their eyes and, from memory, to recall what – for them – are significant Gospel pictures of Jesus. The Leader may begin with the following example, then others can follow the pattern, beginning with the phrase, 'I see Jesus ...':

Leader: I see Jesus ...
sitting in a boat looking at the crowds of people
who have come to hear him.

It may be helpful to sing the chant BEHOLD THE LAMB OF GOD – see Appendix, page 113 – before and after each remembrance. The Leader may end the meditation by saying:)

Leader: Thanks be to God who has met us in Jesus.
ALL: AMEN.

Invitation

Celebrant: This is the table,
not of the Church, but of the Lord.
It is to be made ready
for those who love him
and who want to love him more.

So, come,
you who have much faith
and you who have little,
you who have been here often
and you who have not been for a long time,
you who have tried to follow
and you who have failed.

Come,
not because it is I who invite you:
it is our Lord.
It is his will that those who want him
should meet him here.

95

Communion song

(During which the bread and wine are brought forward)

The story

Celebrant: Now let us hear the story
of how this sacrament began.

Reader: On the night on which Jesus was betrayed,
he sat at supper with his disciples.
While they were eating, he took a piece of bread,
said a blessing,
broke it and gave it to them with the words,
'This is my body. It is broken for you.
Do this to remember me.'

Later, he took a cup of wine, saying,
'This cup is God's new covenant,
sealed with my blood.
Drink from it, all of you, to remember me.'

Celebrant: So now, following Jesus' example and command,
we take this bread and this wine,
the ordinary things of the world
which Christ will make special.
And as he said a prayer before sharing,
let us do so too.

Eucharistic prayer A

Leader: As we approach sharing Communion with our Lord,
let us express our gratitude to God
for what is important to us at this time,
whether that be ordinary or special.

In this prayer I shall say two phrases,
each ending with 'Thank you, God,'
to which we all respond,
'THANK YOU, GOD.'

After that, anyone else may give thanks,
using the same pattern

and ending with the same words
which we all repeat.

Let us pray.

For this time and this place
and those around us,
thank you, God

ALL: THANK YOU, GOD.

Leader: For our freedom to worship
and name you,
thank you, God.

ALL: THANK YOU, GOD.

*(Others may follow in the same pattern ad lib, until the
Leader reads the sentence before the SANCTUS)*

Eucharistic prayer B

Leader: Gratitude, praise,
hearts lifted high,
voices full and joyful ...
these you deserve.

For when we were nothing,
you made us something.
When we had no name
and no faith and no future,
you called us your children.
When we lost our way or turned away,
you did not abandon us.
When we came back to you,
your arms opened wide in welcome.

And look,
you prepare a table for us
offering not just bread, not just wine,
but your very self
so that we may be filled, forgiven,
healed, blessed and made new again.
You are worth all our pain and all our praise.

So now, in gratitude,
we join our voices
to those of the Church on earth and in heaven:

Sanctus   *(Spoken or sung – see Appendix, page 126)*

ALL: HOLY, HOLY, HOLY LORD,
GOD OF POWER AND MIGHT.
HEAVEN AND EARTH ARE FULL OF YOUR GLORY.
HOSANNA IN THE HIGHEST.

BLESSED IS HE WHO COMES
IN THE NAME OF THE LORD.
HOSANNA IN THE HIGHEST.

Leader: Lord God,
as we come to share the richness of your table,
we cannot forget the rawness of the earth.

We cannot take bread
and forget those who are hungry.
Your world is one world
and we are stewards of its nourishment.

ALL: LORD, PUT OUR PROSPERITY
AT THE SERVICE OF THE POOR.

Leader: We cannot take wine
and forget those who are thirsty.
The ground and the rootless,
the earth and its weary people cry out for justice.

ALL: LORD, PUT OUR FULLNESS
AT THE SERVICE OF THE EMPTY.

Leader: We cannot hear your words of peace
and forget the world at war
or, if not at war, then preparing for it.

ALL: SHOW US QUICKLY, LORD,
HOW TO TURN WEAPONS
INTO WELCOME SIGNS
AND THE LUST FOR POWER
INTO A DESIRE FOR PEACE.

Leader: We cannot celebrate the feast of your family
and forget our divisions.
We are one in spirit, but not in fact.
History and hurt still dismember us.

ALL: LORD, HEAL YOUR CHURCH
IN EVERY BROKENNESS.

Prayer of consecration

Celebrant: For us you were born,
for us you healed,
preached, taught
and showed the way to heaven;
for us you were crucified,
and for us, after death,
you rose again.

Lord Jesus Christ,
present with us now,
for all that you have done
and all that you have promised,
what have we to offer?

Our hands are empty,
our hearts are sometimes full of wrong things.
We are not fit to gather up the crumbs
from under your table.

But with you is mercy
and the power to change us.

So as we do in this place
what you did in an upstairs room,
send down your Holy Spirit
on us
and on these gifts of bread and wine
that they may become for us your body,
healing, forgiving
and making us whole;

and that we may become,
for you,
your body,
loving and caring in the world
until your kingdom comes.
Amen.

(Taking and breaking the bread)

Among friends, gathered round a table,
Jesus took bread, broke it and said,
'This is my body,
  it is broken for you.'

(Taking the cup of wine)

And later he took the cup of wine and said,
'This is the new relationship with God,
  made possible because of my death.
Take this – all of you – to remember me.'

(Spoken or sung – see Appendix, page 111)

ALL: LAMB OF GOD,
YOU TAKE AWAY THE SIN OF THE WORLD,
HAVE MERCY UPON US.

LAMB OF GOD,
YOU TAKE AWAY THE SIN OF THE WORLD,
HAVE MERCY ON US.

LAMB OF GOD,
YOU TAKE AWAY THE SIN OF THE WORLD,
GRANT US YOUR PEACE.

Celebrant: Look,
here is your Lord coming to you
in bread and wine.

These are the gifts of God
for the people of God.

(The bread and wine are shared according to appropriate custom. A quiet chant may be sung as the elements are distributed.)

The Peace

Celebrant: Please stand.

Not an easy peace,
not an insignificant peace,
not a half-hearted peace,
but the peace of the Lord Jesus Christ
is with us now.

Let us share it with each other.

(The PEACE may be shared)

Concluding prayer

Leader: Lord Jesus Christ,
you have put your life into our hands;
now we put our lives into yours.

Take us,
renew and remake us.
What we have been is past;
what we shall be, through you,
still awaits us.

Lead us on.
Take us with you.

ALL: AMEN.

Closing song *(ALL standing)*

Closing responses

Leader:	The cross,
ALL:	WE SHALL TAKE IT;
Leader:	the bread,
ALL:	WE SHALL BREAK IT;
Leader:	the pain,
ALL:	WE SHALL BEAR IT;
Leader:	the joy,
ALL:	WE SHALL SHARE IT;
Leader:	the Gospel,
ALL:	WE SHALL LIVE IT;
Leader:	the love,
ALL:	WE SHALL GIVE IT;
Leader:	the light,
ALL:	WE SHALL CHERISH IT;
Leader:	the darkness,
ALL:	GOD SHALL PERISH IT.

Liturgy for a service of healing

It is envisaged that this liturgy will not happen in isolation. People should never be confronted with a service of healing simply because someone in authority thinks it would be a good or a novel thing. Where people have never been introduced to the Church's ministry of healing, time should be taken for preparation and discussion.

This liturgy is not intended for services in which the charismatic gifts of a few individuals will be shared, but where the Church in all its frailty obeys Christ's will and command that hands should be laid on those who suffer, and prayer made for them.

There should be a clearly designated area where people may kneel and hands be laid upon them both by the Leader(s) of worship and others standing behind. This may be at communion rails around the altar, or it may be at kneelers in a circle round a cross and some candles. Alternatively, in a small group, people may prefer to have a vacant chair on which they may sit.

If candles are to be lit in association with the prayers, that should happen at a safe distance from where people gather to lay on hands.

Opening responses   *(ALL standing)*

Leader: O God, who created the heavens
             and stretched them out,
ALL: WE PRAISE YOU!
Leader: You fashioned the earth and all that lives there,
ALL: WE PRAISE YOU!
Leader: You give breath to the people upon it,
             and Spirit to those who walk on it.
ALL: WE PRAISE AND THANK YOU, O GOD!
Leader: That the eyes of the blind be opened,
             the broken-hearted be healed,
             the poor hear the good news,
             the captives be brought out of darkness,
ALL: YOUR KINGDOM COME, O LORD.
             YOUR WILL BE DONE.

Leader: So shall we sing a new song, O Lord,
ALL: AND PRAISE YOUR NAME FOR EVER.

Song or hymn

Prayer *(ALL sit)*

Leader: Let us pray.

As if it were not enough
to bring sound from silence,
    light from darkness,
    order from confusion;
as if it were not enough
to make the world excellent and intricate,
you gave the kiss of life to the dust of the earth.
You made male and female,
me and us.
ALL: SO WE BLESS YOU.

Leader: As if it were not enough
to watch the world you had created,
to admire your handwork from eternity;
as if it were not enough
to care and be kind at a distance,
you sent your Son to be flesh of our flesh,
bone of our bone,
to live and walk beside
me and us.
ALL: SO WE BLESS YOU.

Leader: As if it were not enough
to be looked at and listened to,
    criticised and complimented,
    feted and forsaken,
you stretched out your arm and held out your hand
to heal and to help
me and us.
ALL: SO WE BLESS YOU.

Leader: As if it were not enough
to do all this and return, triumphant, to glory,

you still hear our cries in the courts of high heaven,
and promise your Spirit for the healing of the nations
and for me and for us.

ALL: SO WE BLESS YOU,
GOD OF ALL POWER,
LORD OF OUR WEAKNESS,
SPIRIT OF OUR SALVATION.
AMEN.

Word of God

*(A scripture reading depicting an aspect of God's love or
Christ's healing ministry is read or enacted, at the
conclusion of which the rubric is shared)*

Leader: This is the Word/Gospel of the/our Lord.
ALL: THANKS BE TO GOD.

Reflection or testimony

*(Someone may offer a short reflection on the above
reading or give some brief personal testimony to God's
healing in his/her experience)*

Prayers for healing

*(If the Leader has previously gathered and categorised
names for intercession these may be read by one or two
others. Otherwise, those present may name aloud
people who are brought to mind during the prayer)*

Leader: O Christ our Lord,
as in times past,
not all the sick and suffering
found their way to your side,
but had to have their hands taken,
or their bodies carried,
or their names mentioned.
So we, confident of your goodness,
bring others to you.

As in times past,
you looked at the faith of friends
and let peace and healing be known.
Look on our faith,
even our little faith

ALL: AND LET YOUR KINGDOM COME.

Leader: We name before you
those for whom pain is the greatest problem;
who are remembered more for their distress
than their potential;
who at night cry, 'I wish to God it were morning,'
and in the morning cry, 'I wish to God it were night.'

*(Here, names may be said aloud, after which the spoken
response may be used or substituted by the chant GOD
TO ENFOLD YOU – see Appendix, page 118)*

Leader: Lord Jesus Christ, Lover of all,
ALL: BRING HEALING, BRING PEACE.

Leader: We name before you
those whose problem is psychological;
those haunted by the nightmares of their past
or the spectres of their future;
those whose minds are shackled
to neuroses, depression or fears,
who do not know what is wrong
or what to pray.

*(Names may be mentioned aloud followed by spoken or
sung response as above)*

Leader: We name before you
those in whose experience
light has turned to darkness,
as the end of a life
or the breaking of a relationship
leaves them stunned in their souls
and silent in their conversation,
not knowing where to turn
or whom to turn to
or whether life has a purpose any more.

(Names may be mentioned aloud followed by spoken or sung response as above)

Leader: And others whose troubles we do not know
or whose names we would not say aloud,
we mention now in the silence
which you understand.

(A silence, followed by spoken or sung response as above)

Leader: Lord God,
you alone are skilled to know the cure
for every sickness and every soul.
If, by our lives, your grace may be known
then in us, through us,
and, if need be, despite us,
ALL: LET YOUR KINGDOM COME.

Leader: On all who tend the sick,
counsel the distressed,
sit with the dying,
or advance medical research
we ask your blessing,
that in caring for your people
they may meet and serve their Lord.

For those who, in this land,
administer the agencies of health and welfare,
we ask your guidance that in all they do
human worth may be valued,
and the service of human need be fully resourced.

This we ask in the name of him
whose flesh and blood
have made all God's children special.
ALL: AMEN.

(If people wish, a chant may be sung here and those who so desire may light a candle in a designated area, remembering the person or persons for whom they have prayed)

Invitation

Leader: During the next song,
those who wish to receive the laying on of hands
should come forward at the last verse
and kneel (or sit) at the appropriate place.

When hands have been laid
and prayer said,
the kneelers (or chair) should be left vacant
for others who want to follow.

Song or hymn

*(During the final verse people move forward and kneel
or sit as appropriate)*

Prayer

Leader: Look, Lord, on your children,
who love your name and need your care.
Let your hands be known
in the touch of friends.

ALL: LORD, SAY THE WORD
AND WE SHALL BE HEALED.

The laying on of hands

*(In turn, hands are laid on those who kneel or sit and
this or a similar prayer is said by the Leader or by all)*

SPIRIT OF THE LIVING GOD,
PRESENT WITH US NOW,
ENTER YOU, BODY, MIND AND SPIRIT,
AND HEAL YOU OF ALL THAT HARMS YOU.
IN JESUS' NAME.
AMEN.

*(After all who require THE LAYING ON OF HANDS
have received this ministry, the following prayer of St
Augustine is said)*

Prayer

Leader: Watch now, dear Lord,
with those who wake
or watch
or weep tonight,
and give your angels charge
over those who sleep.

Tend your sick ones, O Lord Christ,
rest your weary ones,
bless your dying ones,
soothe your suffering ones,
pity your afflicted ones,
shield your joyous ones,
and all for your love's sake.

Now may the God of hope fill us
with all joy and peace in believing,
that we may abound in hope
in the power of the Holy Spirit.

ALL: AMEN.

Song or hymn

(During which all resume their seats)

The Grace

ALL: THE GRACE OF OUR LORD JESUS CHRIST,
THE LOVE OF GOD,
AND THE FELLOWSHIP OF THE HOLY SPIRIT
BE WITH US ALL,
EVERMORE.
AMEN.

Appendix

Agnus Dei / Lamb of God (St Bride setting)

Music by John L. Bell © 1995 WGRG, Iona Community, Glasgow G51 3UU, Scotland

Alleluia (Duncan)

Music by Norah Duncan IV © 1987 GIA Publications, Inc., 7404 S. Mason Ave., Chicago, IL 60638, USA. All rights reserved.

Behold the Lamb of God

Music by John L. Bell © 1988 WGRG, Iona Community, Glasgow G51 3UU, Scotland

Come, Holy Spirit

Music by John L. Bell © 1995 WGRG, Iona Community, Glasgow G51 3UU, Scotland

- na - tha! ____

MA - RA - NA - THA! ____

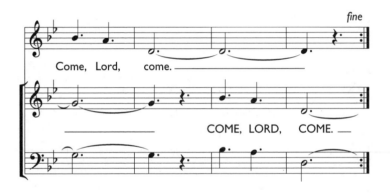

fine

Come, Lord, come. ____

COME, LORD, COME. ____

Gloria (Iona)

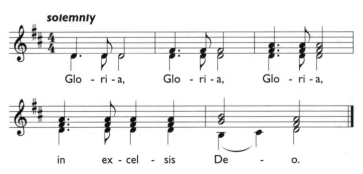

solemnly

Glo - ri - a, Glo - ri - a, Glo - ri - a,

in ex - cel - sis De - o.

Traditional

Gloria (Peruvian)

Public domain

Al - le - lu - ia! A - men! *(Group 1)*

AL - LE - LU - IA! A - MEN!

Al - le - lu - ia! A - men! *(Group 2)*

AL - LE - LU - IA! A - MEN! AL - LE - LU - IA! A - MEN!

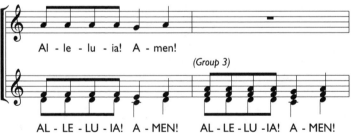

Al - le - lu - ia! A - men! *(Group 3)*

AL - LE - LU - IA! A - MEN! AL - LE - LU - IA! A - MEN!

AL - LE - LU - IA! A - MEN! AL - LE - LU - IA! A - MEN!——

117

God to enfold you

Words & music by John L. Bell © 1995 WGRG, Iona Community,
Glasgow G51 3UU, Scotland

sight; so may God grace you,

heal and em - brace you, lead you through

dark - ness in - to the light.

Halle, halle, halle

Melody Caribbean traditional; arrangement by John L. Bell © 1990 WGRG,
Iona Community, Glasgow G51 3UU, Scotland

Jesus Christ, Jesus Christ

Words & music by John L. Bell © 1998 WGRG, Iona Community, Glasgow G51
3UU, Scotland

Jesus Christ, Son of God

slowly

Cantor:

Je - sus Christ, Son of God, have

ALL:

mer - cy up - on us. JE - SUS CHRIST,

SON OF GOD, HAVE MER - CY UP - ON US.

Music by John L. Bell © 1987 WGRG, Iona Community, Glasgow G51 3UU, Scotland

Listen, Lord

gently

Lis - ten, Lord, lis - ten, Lord, not to our words but to our prayer. You a - lone, you a - lone un - der - stand and care.

Words & music by John L. Bell & Graham Maule © 1989 WGRG, Iona Community, Glasgow G51 3UU, Scotland

Lord, draw near

Words & music by John L. Bell © 1987 WGRG, Iona Community,
Glasgow G51 3UU, Scotland

Lord, in your mercy

Music by John L. Bell © 1995, 1998 WGRG, Iona Community,
Glasgow G51 3UU, Scotland

Sanctus and Benedictus (St Bride setting)

Music by John L. Bell © 1995 WGRG, Iona Community, Glasgow G51 3UU, Scotland